MISSISSIPPI VERSE

MISSISSIPPI VERSE

EDITED BY
ALICE JAMES

CHAPEL HILL
THE UNIVERSITY OF NORTH CAROLINA PRESS
1934

COPYRIGHT, 1934, BY
THE UNIVERSITY OF NORTH CAROLINA PRESS

PRINTED IN THE UNITED STATES OF AMERICA BY
THE SEEMAN PRESS, DURHAM, NORTH CAROLINA
THIS BOOK WAS DIGITALLY PRINTED.

To

MY PARENTS
LORENZO JAMES
ALICE MURRAY JAMES

AND TO

MY BROTHER
LORENZO JAMES, JR.

ACKNOWLEDGMENTS

IT IS A PLEASURE to acknowledge my indebtedness to Dr. Calvin S. Brown, Professor of Modern Languages at the University of Mississippi, Dr. David H. Bishop, Professor of English at the University of Mississippi, and Dr. A. P. Hudson, Associate Professor of English at the University of North Carolina, for their many helpful suggestions and encouraging interest; and to the authors represented in this book.

A number of these poems have already been published and for permission to reprint them thanks are due to the editors of *The American Mercury, Poetry, The Christian Science Monitor, The North American Review, New Republic, Commonweal, The Lyric, Harpers Magazine, Current Literature, Scribner's Magazine, Bozart and Contemporary Verse, The English Journal, The Missionary Voice, The New York Times, The Journal* of Southern Methodist University, and the *Sylvester Memorial* (The Principia, St. Louis), and to the following publishers: Harrison Smith & Robert Haas, Inc., Harold Vinal, Henry Harrison, Charles Scribner's Sons, The Yale University Press, and the Publishing House of the Methodist Episcopal Church South.

ALICE JAMES.

University, Mississippi
January, 1934.

Table of Contents

	PAGE
INTRODUCTION BY ARTHUR PALMER HUDSON	xi
LEMUELLA ALMOND	3
ELIZABETH AUSTIN	4
RODNEY M. BAINE	6
KATHRYN BARINGER	6
JULIA S. BLUNDELL	8
THOMAS T. BRACKIN	10
NEZZIE JEANETTE BRASWELL	12
CALVIN S. BROWN III	14
LOIS BROWN	15
MAUD MORROW BROWN	16
ALEX HEAD BURNETT	17
MARY EFFIE CAMERON	17
CHARLOTTE CHAMPENOIS	19
ADA NEILL CLARK	22
HORACE POLK COOPER	23
HUBERT CREEKMORE	25
ADELE DE LA BARRE	28
WILLIAM FAULKNER	31
FRANCES GIBSON	35
SANFORD CHARLES GLADDEN	37
YVONNE GRAHAM	38
EVELYN HAMMETT	41
HARRIET RICE HARNED	43
JAMIE SEXTON HOLME	44
ARTHUR PALMER HUDSON	46
MARJORIE JACKSON	48

	PAGE
MUNA LEE	51
GLADYS BROOKRESON LEGG	54
CATHERINE NAOMI MCFARLANE	55
NELLE GRAVES MCGILL	57
FREDERIC FRANCIS MELLEN	61
MARY LESLIE NEWTON	62
G. MARION O'DONNELL	67
WILLIAM ALEXANDER PERCY	69
TALLULAH RAGSDALE	73
KITTY REID	74
JESSA SOPER	76
AUBREY STARKE	76
PAUL MONTREVILLE WEST	78
STELLA MUSE WHITEHEAD	81
KUMMER WRINN	82
STARK YOUNG	83
RACHEL ZELLER	85
BIOGRAPHICAL NOTES	87

INTRODUCTION

THE EDITOR'S AIM has been to give wide representation to present-day poetic effort and achievement by authors native of the state or resident in the state or both. All the pieces belong to the twentieth century; poems by older writers like Irwin Russell and Walter Malone have been omitted. The authors range from young people still in school or college to middle-aged men and women of the world. The widest extremes of literary experience are indicated in the brief biographical sketches. A few of the authors, like Stark Young and William Faulkner, are professional (and successful) men of letters. A few, as, for example, William A. Percy and Muna Lee, are people of affairs who pursue literature as an avocation. A few are mature men and women who write occasional verse as an intellectual diversion and solace from busy lives as teachers, lawyers, housewives, and artists. Many are students just achieving articulate expression.

There is in the anthology a corresponding range of literary merit. Some of the pieces (as Miss James's notes show) have enjoyed the distinction of publication in the best periodicals of this country; a few have appeared in books bearing the imprimatur of time-honored presses or firms. But most of them have never been published. Miss James is to be congratulated for obtaining authors' and publishers' permission to reprint pieces by writers of distinction side by side with pieces by amateurs. And these skilled craftsmen are to be congratulated on their democratic willingness to associate between these boards with their younger brothers and sisters of the arts.

Lovers of poetry are little concerned about time and place. Few such, looking into this little volume, will have predilections for or prejudices against Mississippi. So life is realized intensely and represented with passion and imagination, or even viewed and reported freshly, with fancy or humor or feeling, they will care little about its local habitat or the name thereof. Yet they may, on second thought, wonder whether the name of the state has any significance in the title.

If so, they will be gratified, negatively at least, by the absence from this volume of any note of shrill sectionalism or blatant local patriotism. They will hear of the siege of Troy, but not of the siege of Vicksburg.

But they will find something of the feel of the land, some features of its known and familiar landscape. Lemuella Almond conveys the virginal beauty of springtime in the Pontotoc and Oxford hill country. In "River Road," Elizabeth Austin communicates the heavy somnolence of a summer night in the Delta. Adele de la Barre has seen autumn in New England and in Mississippi, and she is poetically aware of the difference. As keenly as she feels the "ecstasy of color" and the "pagan glory" which sent the Pilgrim fathers to their knees, so delicately she responds to the "new tenderness" in hibiscus, jasmine, and lantana in some old garden on Mississippi Sound. Maud Morrow Brown dreams of the sedge-grass fields "And their dull gold shining soft through slanting silver shafts of rain." Marjorie Jackson's memory is etched with the image of pines that "go down to meet the sea" at Biloxi or Pass Christian. Mary Leslie Newton's "The Levees" dramatizes effectively the nightmare of those who sleep o' nights in rooms below the level of the yellow Mississippi at swirling flood times. She mythifies prettily the Queen Anne's lace that trims many a winding country road. William Alexander Percy's nostalgic inward eye gazes

> Across flat fields that love and touch the sky.
> ....
> Soon now the peace of summer will be there
> With cloudy fire of myrtles in full bloom;
> And when the marvelous wide evenings come,
> Across the molten river, one can see
> The misty willow-green of Arcady.

Being a real poet, Mr. Percy of course might have seen the "misty willow-green" across the Ohio or the Danube or any other noble river in the world; but it is one of the indigenous touches of this little volume that he saw it—near Greenville, perhaps—across Delta fields, a levee, and the Mississippi. And there are many other such, no less true and poetic for being allusive or incidental.

Whether for better or for worse, the reader will find little or no conscious social criticism of conditions especially characteristic of Mississippi. That note accords little with the lyric strain which dominates the volume. Most of the authors take or leave their people as they find them. Adele de la Barre's "Lines to a Little Town," expressing a sense of spiritual suffocation in the stuffy religiosity and morality of a village, is certainly true of many a Mississippi community, but so is it of Gopher Prairie and Sauk Center. Nezzie Jeanette Braswell's "The City"—a composite of, say, Hattiesburg and Memphis—shows a mild awareness of the barbarity of many an over-grown country town. Marjorie Jackson looks with tolerant amusement on the lazy-bones sleeping in the sun-drenched courthouse square of Oxford—cur and nag and loafer, all blissfully forgetful that their sires had been, respectively, foxhounds, race-horses, and gentlemen, in the golden age. On the whole, as in Miss de la Barre's "Nigger Jig," the attitude of these poets toward their *milieu* is light-hearted and unreflective. Most of the things they say or hint about it are kindly. Mr. Percy, having "need of silence and of stars," dazed by "too much . . . said too loudly," bethinks him of "men as earnest and less shrill," and longs to go

> Back to the more of earth, the less of man,
> Where there is still a plain simplicity,
> And friendship, poor in everything but love,
> And faith, unwise, unquestioned, but a star.

Though there is some sensitive perception and notation of physical and social aspects of life in Mississippi, the great majority of these pieces are neither intentionally nor unintentionally regional. They bespeak interests and tastes characteristic of observant and thoughtful, well-read and reflective young people everywhere in the United States.

A few pieces show imaginative preoccupation with the past in myth and history. Calvin S. Brown III hears the (somewhat Miltonic) voices of the Christian martyrs across the gulf of the ages. Above the bloody clamor of the circus they "heard the hymnings of a heavenly choir" and the "avenging thunders of their God"; now, in the impartiality of dust, they sleep, forgotten of that God, among princes and infidels who mocked them. Tallulah Ragsdale maintains that, for moving appeal, Percival's white innocence was as naught to Launcelot's penitential sorrow. Aubrey Starke indulges in light speculation upon the after-courses of Helen of Troy, in a manner faintly reminiscent of Mr. John Erskine.

The impact of scientific progress upon the poetic imagination is the theme of a number of poems. Hubert Creekmore's irregular sonnet "Before a Leyden Jar" is a prayer to the "great god of volts and joules"—a bitter, ironic cry of one who seeks once more to mold the shape of our lost world "from lifeless bits to singing awe," and only faintly hopes that with more of knowledge (and perhaps of reverence) he may "weave wreaths of stars, and breathe the weird perfume they drop." In his "Boy and Eagle" William Faulkner follows a young and unspoiled Babbitt who, watching a soaring airplane, projected his boyish imagination into the blue and

> . . . saw the fleeing canyons of the sky
> Tilt to banshee wire and slanted aileron,
> And his own lonely shape on scudding walls
> Where harp the ceaseless thunders of the sun.

Written for the most part by young people, many of these verses express more or less articulately the divine discontent of youth, or anticipations of disillusionment. Marjorie Jackson's "Non Credo" is eloquent of youth's skepticisms. Kummer Wrinn's "Anathema," original in its expression, is Shelleyan in its smouldering revolt against creed, custom, and convention. More mature in experience, perhaps, as in expression, Mr. Percy's treatment of the theme is most poignant of all:

> ....The harbors of the past,
> Silted, have grown too shallow for our deepening keels;

and though with the laughter of June, the heart gives heed again—

> But, ah, for youth that is fled,
> Fled, with all but its pain.

As might be expected, the majority of the contributions are by women. The variety of themes peculiarly feminine is great. Jamie Sexton Holme's "Preparedness" foresees

> . . . the fate that comes to one
> Who gives her whole heart to a child.

Mary Leslie Newton's "Sestina of the Dead Mother" with haunting pathos pursues the theme of frustrated maternal love beyond the grave. Nelle Graves McGill's "My Daughter Dreams" is an exquisite study of child life. The same author's "Reservation" and Marjorie Jackson's "Woman's Love" boldly assert that the inner citadel of a woman's soul can neither be surrendered nor violated. Jessa Soper's "When You Fall in Love" slyly predicts that the process will have been "planned so carefully . . . you'll say, 'It's fate'." "Daffodils," by Yvonne Graham, conceals a broken heart under the persiflage of a game of bridge.

A few pieces will be found to escape any attempt at suggestive classification of themes. They will please, perhaps, by their boldness of conception, or by the virtuosity of execution, or sometimes by both. If they are not, in Mr. Oliver Elton's phrase, "epigrams in the highest sense—a complete and immortal utterance of a single passing thought or emotion," they at least have qualities of the fine epigram. Such are two by Stark Young—one beginning "There shall be no day empty of you" and the other entitled "To a Rose at a Window of Heaven." Such is William Alexander Percy's

"To C. P." Brevity and sharpness of outline are characteristics of Frances Gibson's "Storm," an Ariel-like rain myth, and Muna Lee's superb images of the flamingo and the raven in "Tropic Dawn." In "Joy" Jamie Sexton Holme, catching her skill, no doubt, from her image, safely trips with her burden of thought across a gossamer thread of verse—

> Joy is but a tight-rope
> Over an abyss!

The casual reader, who sometimes hesitates between thumbing and not thumbing through such a volume, and who might be grateful for some such hints of subject matter as have been given, would doubtless be bored by further attempts to indicate the variety of other themes treated. And so with any attempt to describe the varieties of verse forms employed, or the levels and features of style exhibited. If, attracted by the novelty of an anthology of verse from Mississippi, and encouraged by this account of what it contains to examine it, the reader ventures into the book, he will prefer to settle critical questions for himself. He will be his own judge as to how far some of the pieces observe the best traditions of English verse, how good or how bad is the poetic nourishment upon which the young have fed, how far the authors are conscious of twentieth-century poetic technique, and what degree of original power has been achieved by a few—in short, what level of poetic talent and taste and cultivation a considerable number of people in Mississippi have attained.

Readers who expect least from Mississippi may fairly experience a gratifying surprise. Whoever reads the volume with just consideration of its aim and with a sympathetic attitude toward its large number of young verse-makers will have recompense in the pleasure of observing attempts at self-expression and in the hopefulness of such exercise. Furthermore, in those pieces which bear the unmistakable accent of poetry, he will enjoy the princely gift which precludes condescension on the part of the receiver.

ARTHUR PALMER HUDSON.

Chapel Hill, North Carolina.

MISSISSIPPI VERSE

Lemuella Almond

HOME HILLS

And may I sing my Mississippi hills?
For long my heart has ached with the desire
To sing home hills, where dogwood blossoms laugh,
White-lipped and cool at April's pausing feet;
Where redbuds flaunt their purple-red beneath
The southern sun, who warms and coaxes them
To be the first gay comers on the hills;
Where fuzzy, gray-green pussy-willows wave
Brown branches, swaying slow to spring's sweet breath.
Home hills, where blue flags bloom at Easter-tide
To speak of God, and gold-cupped touch-me-nots
Come trooping down the spring-fed brooks to charm
The barefoot child; where happy bluebirds sing
Among the leaf-robed trees, and whip-poor-wills
Call plaintively on starry nights. To you,
Fair hills of home, I give my meed of praise.
Dear hills, vine-clad, red hills, and valleys wide,
Where winding rivers run by low sweet fields
Of tasselling corn laid by in June, and on
Through meadows twinkling white with clover blooms;
Or slip beneath the tangled roofs of leaves
In primal wood where timid wild things feed
And drink and scamper all day unafraid—
Forever I could sing of you, and yet
Contentment I shall never find. My words

Cannot express the pride I feel, the joy
I know, when bluebirds build about my house,
Where apple-blossoms drift and children play.

Elizabeth Austin

RED ROSE

I gave my love a red rose,
A rose with fragrant lips,
And laughter sparkled through me
Down to my finger tips.

But O, my golden happiness
Has melted into air.
I saw my love's new sweetheart
With a red rose in her hair!

THE RIVER ROAD

The moon is hanging low tonight,
A lonely little lantern,
That gleams a faint, pale yellow
In the blue-black sky.
The white magnolia blossoms
Lift their heavy heads to listen,
While through the darkness
Comes the whip-poor-will's far cry.
The bull-frog in the marshes
Splashes through the unseen water;
He croaks a mournful serenade
And mocks the leaping gars.

The quiet river ripples,
A plaintive banjo tinkles,
And blinking ferry lamp-lights
Wink in answer to the stars.

SECRETS

Sometimes I wish that I might be
So gay and debonair,
That I could laugh at trivial things,
And wear exotic gowns and rings,
And swish a heavy feathered fan,
Or even dye my hair;
And not lament especially
What my small world might say
If I should leave my peaceful home,
And tiresome little tasks, to roam
The unknown roads that call to me
Some lovely April day.

But who am I to think at all,
Of incense smoke or peacock fans,
Of woodlands pink with buds in spring,
Or caravans,—or anything
But ruffled curtains, firesides bright,
And shining pots and pans?

My quiet neighbors never know
My dreams of lands, and flags unfurled.
I trim the roses on the lawn,
And only in the silver dawn
I long to laugh at life, and tie
A big red ribbon 'round the world.

Rodney M. Baine

REQUIEM

Slowly and with due reverence
Fill up the grave.
And you who with benevolence
Look upon me, to whom he gave
Life, look not in pity. Not for me
Is pity due or right.
I do not desire it. Do not you see
Me unmoved at even this sight?
You are amazed, perhaps, at what you find?
His son, without a tear . . . and yet,
What are prayers to a Higher Mind
For eternal happiness? Best forget.
He would not wish for unending life,
Spent in grey hairs, kneeling round a throne,
Raising hymns—no more pain, no strife,
Naught but praising God. For he had known
Life in his youth, and in that life anew begun,
Even now he lives and knows the strength of youth.
His hair no longer grey, he lives in me, his son;
And this, not life eternal, is the rejoicing truth.

Kathryn Baringer

EXPLANATION

I would not show you any more
The steadfast ways I know
Or fumble at your heavy door,

But silently would go
Into a wider place. But oh,
The world is cramped into
This lonely, pebbled little road
Leading up to you.

IN A ROOM ALONE

Oh, I could bear my heart to break
In a room, alone,
With not a window looking out,
And not a door, not one;

With not a footstep in the hall;
Nobody come to peer,
And not a soul to sit with me,
And not a voice to hear.

Oh, I could bear my heart to break
In a room, alone,
With only pride to stare at me—
With only pride of stone.

CONFESSION

Being good seemed such a pretty thing,
I thought I'd like to be
A tall white nun in a cool white cell.
(Holy Father, pray for me.)

I've told my lover a cold farewell,
My mother shall see me no more.
I have not minded the cold hard bed
Nor the stone uncarpeted floor.

But tonight on the shining breast of the moon
(Holy Father, pray for me)
I wept for the golden hair I once had,
Which my lover loved to see.

Tonight on the golden breast of the moon
(Holy Father, hear my prayer)
I wept for the shining hair I once had.
(The Mother of God had long bright hair.)

Julia S. Blundell

I SAW A PENCIL SKETCH OF DEATH

I saw a pencil sketch of death today.
The gray lead lines were clear, were somehow cold
And strangely strong;—the figure, gnarled but bold,
Was hidden underneath full folds of gray,
And showed no feature but his hollow eyes.
One felt almost his icy, blue-cold breath,
Almost discerned the skinny hand of death
And almost heard his low successive sighs.
Death cannot be like that,—this death renowned.
His icy breath of penetrating fright
Is rather one of freshness, cold and pure,
Prophetic not of prisons underground
Nor darkness, but of color and of light,
Adventure and mysterious allure.

THE PUPPET MAKER

He sat upon a bench of maple wood,
That, like himself, showed marks of many years.

Around him all his tools in chaos stood:
His paints, his brushes, and his sharpened shears.
His eyes shone so, one thought of glowing fires;
They showed oblivion of the world about—
Their dark, dilated pupils prophesiers
Of all the roguish puppets he carves out—
Mere puppets, bits of wood shaped with a knife,
And hung, haphazardly, on thick, white strings—
Mere toys, to which belongs no spark of life—
Yet his seemed almost breathing, moving things,
And he had used no cunning stratagem . . .
But simply gave his soul to each of them.

STRANGE NIGHT

A silver moon
In a tar-black sky
(Like a ghost's balloon
Or a blind man's eye)
  Rolls, and is still.

An easterly gale
That smells of rain
Wafts the mystic wail
Of a ghost's refrain,
  Piercingly shrill.

Black shadows change
Each shifting cast
Into one more strange,
And stand aghast,
  Shaking with chill.

A leafless bush,
Like a spider gray,
Signals "hush"
In a grotesque way,
    Ready to kill
        With a mad man's skill.

        And the moon shines still.

Thomas Brackin

THE CUP-BEARER

He passed the frothy champagne cup of joy.
His fellow-revelers, a myriad host,
With laughter and with song, drank deep
And cheered him on, with merriment
And many sounding thumps upon his back
In comradery. And then, the cup exhausted,
From his heart he poured the dull, and biting
Heavy wine of pain. The strong remained
To drink. The many shuddering passed it by
And left him drunken with his agony,
And anguish in his eye, a lonely
Silent pride within the soul.

RE-CREATION

O Earth, great common mother of us all,
Upon thy breast I stretch me prone this fair
Spring morning. May thy life-giving power
Which makes all things to grow, to change, to flower,
Flow into me and give me life anew;

Give to my soul that wondrous peace which fills
This valley with its quiet; give my mind
The beauty and the symmetry of even
The simplest flower; make my body strong
And free to do the bidding of a soul
Forever deep in love with thee.

Earth-Mother! As thy wayward child I beg
But of the crumbs of this great feast; make me
Not chief, but humblest of created works
That I may look upon thy face, and, having looked,
Be strong and silent, swift and sure,
As one who feels himself an humble part
Of thy great plan, a tiny thread in that
Eternal tapestry which forms the garment of a God.

REVEILLE

Man's heart is a wild, free thing
Not bound by an age or a zone,
And ever his spirit must leap and sing,
    Mid the din of traffic
    Or by mountain spring
When Freedom calls her own.

Shackled the body and brain may be
To a task for years, and never groan;
But ever the heart that is wild and free
    Must answer the call,
    Respond to the plea
And return to its own.

THE UNCUT CORD

I am a child of Woman
And in days like these
Must find my way
Back to a woman's breast,
And there, a child again,
My head upon her heart,
Sob out my bitter tale
Of broken hopes
And tangled plans
And aspirations all awry,
And then I hear her say,
With soft maternal touch
Upon my head, "Take heart!
My little man. Perhaps
'Twill not be half so bad
Tomorrow."

Nezzie Jeanette Braswell

THE CITY

Along Main Street the crowd mills
Looking for bargains.
Flivvers with shrieking brakes
Halt for red lights, then dash on
Around the corner, searching for
Some one, anyone.

Dazzling show windows, Parisian gowns,
Fur coats, gay prints,
Department stores bulging with crowds,

Markets with roast pig,
Jewelry, radio shops beckoning.

Old men, young men, boys stand on corners
In front of drug stores, leaning against buildings,
Smoking, chewing, spitting on sidewalks,
Spinning smutty yarns, solving world problems,
Complaining, gazing at fair ones, making remarks.

Narrow, dingy, dirty streets
With beggars here and there,
Taxies dodging double-parked cars.
Poor people gathered in knots
Near stinking retail stores
Hoping for better days.

The city, all aglow on Main Street,
Dimmer and duller on the back ones.

DAWN

The fading moon and pale-faced stars
Pull the curtains of night with them to the hills.
From the rose arbor a chorus of birds drifts
From the finale of the night to the prelude of a new day.
Scenes shift o'er the eastern hills;
Pink and orchid fade to orange and gray.
Violets and sleepy primroses bow their dew-laden heads,
To Him for the gift of a new day.

LIFE

Life is like a rose, topped with dew,
Blooming in a rose garden.

At sunrise it is loveliest, a pink tight bud.
Unfolded at noon, it gives its life,
Fragrance, beauty, and cheer.
Fading at twilight, its petals are shed;
Back to the mold it returns....

THE MOON

The new moon, lying on its back,
Stuck on the peak of a western hill;
Momentarily it rested in the cool breeze,
Then dropped from sight.

Calvin S. Brown III

THE MARTYRS

They fell in ashes on the blackened sod
Of Nero's gardens, while about their pyre
The pagans mocked a faith that dared aspire
To life eternal. Neither rack nor rod
Could turn them from the path their Master trod;
They heard the hymning of a heavenly choir,
And louder than the godless tyrant's lyre
Crashed the avenging thunders of their God.
The tumult in the circus died away—
The splendor of the Empire fell in dust—
The catacombs are tenantless, and deep
Beneath the ruins, in the silent clay,
Forgetful of a god who broke his trust,
Beside the priests and infidels, they sleep.

ON HANDEL'S *MESSIAH*

O Sect of Christ, when time's relentless tread
Has crushed your scattered embers into dust;
When gods as yet unknown are held in trust,
And those whom you adored are past and dead;
When you appear before the judgment seat
Of strange historians of stranger creed,
And when your empty claims you vainly plead,
And speak of ransomed souls and sin's retreat;
When your accusers throng about the throne
Proclaiming far and wide your vast misdeeds,
The inquisitions of dissenting creeds—
The shattered lives with which your path is strown;
When heaven and earth accuse, and none defend,
Let Handel speak—not all your works offend!

Lois Brown

I THOUGHT I HEARD YOUR VOICE

I thought I heard your voice; I answered.
But it was just the sad wind murmuring
Above the lost grave of a red rose.
I thought I saw your eyes; I looked up.
But they were just two dawn-paled stars that,
Frightened by the rising brilliance, set.
I thought I felt your hands; I caught them.
But they were just two great white moths that,
Blinded by the half-light, brushed my face.

Maud Morrow Brown

BROOM SEDGE

The hills of Mississippi are very fair in autumn.
The hickory lights a yellow torch in groves of dim green pine;
The black-gum lifts its crimson crest and bronze viburnum berries
Sway where bamboo and bright moon-seed on the sumac bushes twine.
But the fairest of all beauty is the beauty of the broom-sedge
When it flings a tawny carpet over every barren height;
When it tosses golden fringes round the dead brown fields of cotton
And rims each red clay gully with a purple band of light.
How it sways and waves and glimmers over gently curving hill-slopes!
How it flames in fiery billows under every rippling breeze!
Through a wild barbaric riot of the richest autumn color
How it spreads an orange background for the gorgeous, glowing trees!
Though I wander ever farther from the hills of Mississippi,
Yet I dream in fading autumn of the sedge-grass fields again.
Then I see their gleaming glory in the warm November sunshine
And their dull gold shining soft through slanting silver shafts of rain.

Aleck Head Burnett

TO THE MORNING STAR

Prosper, happy must you be
Leading the way,
Springing forth exultingly
At break of day.
Everywhere the world is waking,
Of the dawn new life partaking.
Man and bird and beast together
Rise from beds in house and heather,
As thy massive golden targe,
Flashing from the great world's marge,
Signaling to land and sea,
Proclaims the break of day.
Prosper, happy must you be,
Leading the way.

Mary Effie Cameron

CATALPA TREE

Down thru the damp hot night
Sweet clinging blossoms fall.
Some stick to my face and arms,
And others hang in the air.

I am a forlorn sweetheart waiting there,
Or a mad-cap with tangles in her hair,
Or a dreaming child asleep from play,
Or a shade wandering from the Styx.

COMPENSATION IN AN INSANE ASYLUM

Years she toiled, washed, boiled, ironed linen,
    rich folks' underpinnin'.
She ate cabbage and bread when there was any;
    hungry days were many.

She bore eight frail children (early six graves);
    two left to misbehave.
Now she is Cleopatra in a court of brocade eating peacock tongues
    brought by an adoring slave.

FURTHER IN THE NIGHT

I stand on the edge of the world but can see no further into the night than the grasp of my hand.

I strain my eyes to see behind shadows but can only picture palaces in the empty spaces out there.

INEVITABLE

You are in every man,
Your smile, your voice,
Your eyes, your hands,
God, even your thoughts.

I'd run, but where?
Into the arms of another
Who'd give me your caresses,
Who'd think me his.

LONGING

I wait for my mate;
Though he come not
   The whole night through.

I wait for my mate;
Though my very youth
   Has long gone.

I wait for my mate;
Others would lie with me,
   But I sleep alone.

MY HANDS

My hands have a million scars on them.
They have held the ugly and touched the beautiful.

They greedily grab and lovingly clasp.
They brutally fight and affectionately caress.
They hastily discard and passionately hold.
They drop a thousand stars and feverishly hold a
   little star-dust.
   Stubby, ugly, starving little hands.

Charlotte Champenois

IRIS

I can remember
Iris
Purple-petaled
In the sun.

A brick walk
Bordered
With iris,
One by one.

My blind eyes
Did not see them then.
But now
That love is done,
I can remember
Iris
Purple-petaled
In the sun.

MARCH WIND

There's a lovely song that the March wind sings,
A song of the joy that April brings—
A promise of leaves for bare brown trees,
A song of clover and bumble-bees,
And robins tilting on the eaves.

MINSTRELSY

When the first sweet promise of morning
Stirs in the old pear tree,
My minstrel thrills his gratitude
For the day that is yet to be.
He tilts on the topmost branches
As the sun begins to rise,
From there he flings his threads of praise
Into the red-gold skies.

REVERIE

I close my eyes. I do not see
The bustling city street,
Nor hear the sounds of passing cars,
The shuffling, hurried feet—
But rather to my eye there comes
A scene that hurry quells—
Yellow butterflies that sway
Near Canterbury bells;
The hum of riveters becomes
A swarm of droning bees,
It seems I hear a cardinal's song,
And murmuring winds in trees.
The hurried, bustling city street
I never see at all—
But hollyhocks that primly stand
Along a whitewashed wall.

SONNET

I planned to love you but a little while,
A few short weeks—at most but half a year —
And then to take my leave, and let no tear
Mar the remembered sweetness of your smile.
I thought of you as but a simple child
(You seemed so innocent and sweet, my dear),
And since your eyes were candid, did not fear
That I, by you, should ever be beguiled.
Ah, but the charm of your simplicity
Has filled the emptiness that was my heart;
Your hands hold all of happiness for me—
(My dear, my dear—if we should ever part!)

A little while I planned our love should last
But now I scheme of ways to hold it fast.

WIND SONG

The soft, warm wind of summer sings
Of eerie, half-fantastic things,
Of dragonflies with thin blue wings—
Of sunbeams sailing a lily boat
On a gleaming pool where broad leaves float
And a fish promenades in a Mandarin coat.
The warm sweet wind at morning sings
Of dragon flies with thin blue wings.

Ada Neill Clark

GYPSIE WISHING

Let me walk
With joy in my heart,
.... Peace in my soul,
A song on my lips,
The sun in my hair, ...
And my feet ...
In the dust of the road.

REQUEST OF AN OLD SAILOR

Blow, O Winds,
Against my pine trees,
And I shall hear the swish

Of ocean waves,
And close my eyes
And dream of storms at sea:
Again I'll feel the surge and strength
Of billows,
Again, the toss and dip of breakers free.
The slash and roar of waters
Bring to me,
Or else, . . . I must go to the sea.

Horace Polk Cooper

LO, THE BOOK

The peach-tree close to my bedroom wall
Is whipped and bent by the wintry gale;
Its swaying branches creak and wail;
Across my blind their shadows sprawl
In the moonlight pale.

Moon-magic changes the window-gauze
To a sheet of paper, smooth and white,
Whereon those shadowy brushes write
Mysteriously, with never a pause,
The livelong night.

Flitting across that silken screen,
They weave me words that surely bring
Strange knowledge of many a secret thing—
But who can tell me what they mean?
Not even thou, O King!

THE RUSSET PEAR-TREE STANDS ALONE

The russet pear-tree stands alone
In shrivelled grass by the river edge;
Chill breezes that ripple the yellowing sedge
Are snared in its branches with petulant moan.

I climbed that steep hill to the west
To pluck the medlars ripening there,
Bronzed by the biting autumn air—
Were Beauty but cure for the heart's unrest!

But my eyes were for naught save the wind-swept plains,
Though I spied no chariot journeying fast,
Half-seen through the whirling dust upcast
By his four white horses with jet-black manes.

Nor is solace yet mine through the soothsayer's art,
For the tortoise shell burnt and the melted lead
Have brought me no comfort, but proved, instead,
Fresh twists of the knife in my aching heart.

The barren pear-tree stands alone;
Icy winds howling in wild carouse
Have quenched the fires of those flaming boughs—
Summer's last heritage now is flown.

THE WISTARIA KIOSQUE

Wistaria twines round the harem towers
of the secret palace of Kei;
it floods each chamber with lavender gloom
as with radiance shed from its lanterns of bloom;
   it cannot be torn away
     from its clutch on the crumbling towers.

No silken cord tightening round ivory throat,
no hemp bruising delicate wrist,
ever clasped them so close as the vine grips the towers,
while it weaves of its falling and withering flowers
    a veil of amethyst
    for the sullen face of the moat.

More creepers, far stronger than silken cords,
that shade like a lowering sky . . .
deeds have been done in those darkling rooms,
things have been shrouded by drowning blooms. . . .
    oh, what may be told in a shrug—or a sigh—
    were best never put into words.

Hubert Creekmore

BEFORE A LEYDEN JAR

Let us pray. To our great god of volts
and joules, our bounty patron, genuflex,
burn incense of our thanks, the while he yokes
us with dull cangues, constrictive vexing belts,
and pushes us along the tedious steppes
where lies his manna. Let us jubilate
that at our feet falls all the world, and let
us hide the tears that seek to mold its shape
again from lifeless bits to singing awe.
"If we will venerate your strength, O Lord,
do homage to your virtues, may not we
also weave wreathes of stars and breathe the weird
perfume they drop? In this faint respite trust,
else all your mercies rot to cursing dust."

COINCIDENCE OF BIRDS

The chance might not repeat that there be three,
and that the sky be sunny empty blue,
and that a singing hush imbue the green
of cradling branches with a boundless tune,
and that a helpless peace suffuse my brain.
Unlike birds, more like aeroplanes, they dived
triangular in loops and spins, behaved
as aviators in a charted line.
Martins more than three had been too much—
a simple flock at play; and less, a pair
at mating. And if it nevermore occur,
I shall have seen the three of me to match
a song of motion in the sky. My soul,
my flesh, my brain, that once were welded whole.

EXPLORATION

Not long ago airplanes attacked the sea
and sought to span it in a single flight.
A dozen fell;—then two found victory
and tribute from the nations' vain delight.
The twelve who might have tasted glory's sweets
swirled down to die upon the desert waves,
unfound and soon forgot, while man engraves
bronze tablets to exalt the winner's feats.
Now I say they may have my cheers and blather —
all my ostentations, mob-led clapping.
Anyone can cheer who's good at slapping
champions on the back; but I would rather
save my songs for those that died unhailed—
not those who won, but those who dared and failed.

PRAYER

So, for the sweetmeats we have tasted when
we thought that they were sweets of lovely sin,
and for the waves of memory that sweep
us back to when our hearts did leap—
let us give thanks, and not on sorrow dwell,
that mystic first love's gone. For who can tell . . . ?
The pain that's dead and long away may be
far dearer than the richest gold reality,
because it breathes again in the breath of song
and shines in the mist of a dumb moon through lace trees.
And the song we hear and the moon-mist filigrees
forsake the dregs that loving draws along
and bring us just the wine of ecstasies,
without the agony of bitter lees.

THIEVES

Often have I wished to chain the dawn
below horizon's rim, attenuate
the tranquil moments of its blushing stain
upon the gray, and keep the day at naught.
Too little peace spins in the sun of noon.
The farthest deaths and massacres are mine
to bear before the bodies yet are cool.
The tight-knit world must flinch in every mile
concertedly aghast at each diverse
atrocity. I have my own deep source
of sorrow and would tend its jealous hurt
without encroaching pleas to pay my court
to others' ills. The wind and sun must merge
as solitary mine before they purge.

Adele De La Barre

AUTUMN GARDEN

I

For some reason
One must be quiet in the garden now.
Even the pecan leaves quiver in silence,
And the mulberries whisper,
And sparrows in the chinaberry tree
Listen intently,
As if for the falling of the first berry.

II

Sunlight hovers over the hibiscus flowers
And touches the full brown delicate
    blossoms of jasmine,
And touches the leaves of the lantana,
With a new tenderness.
Not with desire,
Not with unkindly vigor,
But as one with passion abated
Who knows only tenderness.

DREAMER BY THE SHORE

I would rather pit my strength stubbornly against the
    insensate strength of the waters,
Bend gasping to the long pull of oars firm in the oarlocks,
Feel the sun hot upon my neck, hot upon the taut curve
    of my shoulders,
I would rather this weariness than any dreaming.

To what purpose dreaming?
To what purpose does man probe listlessly into the far
    gleaming of starlight—into the surging of tides
    and the silent recession, the quiet of night,
    the peace of the shadow?
To what purpose dreaming?

NIGGER JIG

Oh, the little nigger feet on the pavement beat
With a slide and a boom and a slide, boom, boom.
Such a mischievous beat have the little black feet
As they jig, jig, jiggle on the busy city street!

"What's this!" said the people as they wandered up and
    down,
"What's that!" said the people from the other end of town.
And they gathered in a circle so they'd not be in the way
Of the black feet jiggin', jig jiggin' up and down.
But *then,* the little niggers, they passed the cup around!

Tootle oot, boom boom, tootle oot, boom boom,
Such a mischievous beat have the little black feet
As they jig, jig, jiggle on the busy city street.
Tootle oot, boom, boom. . . .

LINES TO A LITTLE TOWN

You are so smug, so self-content
I wonder that the spring
Will flaunt for you its arrogant
Tempestuous blossoming.

I marvel that the jessamine
And flaming trumpet vine
Can flower near such fear of sin
And such distrust of wine.

SHE DOES NOT LISTEN

We sipped from delicate cups of China tea
With candle light and twilight and the trees
Dark against sky that blossomed like a rose;
And you were deft and charming in your pose
Of housewife queening it 'mongst all of these
Innumerable slim implements for tea,—
Your silver pitchers, and your courtesy
Of "Pardon, is it lemon?" "One lump, please?"
And delicate adjustments such as these
Become so great a ritual that I,
Who had so much about myself to say,
Finished my cup of tea and came away.

NEW ENGLAND AUTUMN

Such ecstasy of color! Such a feast
Of yellow birch and scarlet maple trees!
Small wonder that the Pilgrim fathers ceased
From pious penitence on bended knees,
Seeing this pagan glory everywhere,
And turned, sedately glad, to thankful prayer.

William Faulkner

MIRROR OF YOUTH

"Behold me, in my feathered cap and doublet,
 strutting across this stage that men call living:
 the mirror of all youth and hope and striving.
 Even you, in me, become a grimace."

"Ay, in that belief you too are but a mortal,
 thinking that peace and quietude and silence
 are but the shadows of your little gestures
 upon the wall of breathing that surrounds you."

"Ho, old spectre, solemnly ribbed with wisdom!
 D'ye think that I must feel your dark compulsions
 and flee with kings and queens in whistling darkness?
 I am star, and sun, and moon, and laughter."

"What star is there that falls, with none to watch it?
 What sun is there more permanent than darkness?
 What moon is there that cracks not? ay, what laughter,
 What purse is there that empties not with spending?

"Ho . . . One grows weary, posturing and grinning,
 aping a dream to a house of peopled shadows!
 Ah, 'twas you who stripped me bare and set me
 gibbering at mine own face in a mirror."

"Yes, it is I who, in the world's clear evening
 with a silver star like a rose in a bowl of lacquer,
 when you have played your play and at last are quiet,
 will wait for you with sleep, and you can drown."

THE COURTESAN IS DEAD

The courtesan is dead, for all her subtle ways,
Her bonds are loosed in brittle and bitter leaves;
Her last long backward look's to see who grieves
The imminent night of her reverted gaze.
Another will reign supreme, now she is dead
And winter's lean clean rain sweeps out her room,
For man's delight and anguish: with old new bloom
Crowning his desire, garlanding his head.

Thus the world, turning to cold and death
When swallows empty the blue and drowsy days
And lean rain scatters the ghost of summer's breath—
The courtesan that's dead, for all her subtle ways—
Spring will come! rejoice! But still is there
An old sorrow sharp as woodsmoke on the air.

GREEN IS THE WATER

Green is the water, green
The grave voluptuous music of the sun;
The pale and boneless fingers of a queen
Upon his body stoop and run.

Within these slow cathedraled corridors
Where ribs of sunlight drown
He joins in green caressing wars
With seamaids red and brown
And chooses one to bed upon
And lapped and lulled is he
By dim dissolving music of the sun
Requiemed down through the sea.

IF THERE BE GRIEF

If there be grief, then let it be but rain,
And this but silver grief for grieving's sake,
If these green woods be dreaming here to wake
Within my heart, if I should rouse again.

But I shall sleep, for where is any death
While in these blue hills slumbrous overhead
I'm rooted like a tree? Though I be dead,
This earth that holds me fast will find me breath.

HERE HE STANDS

Here he stands, while eternal evening falls
And it is like a dream between gray walls
Slowly falling, slowly falling
Between two walls of gray and topless stone,
Between two walls with silence on them grown.
The twilight is severed with waters always falling
And heavy with budded flowers that never die,
And a voice that is forever calling
Sweetly and soberly.

Spring wakes the walls of a cold street,
Sows silver remembered seed in frozen places:
Upon meadows like still and simply smiling faces,
And wrinkled streams, and grass that knew her feet.

Here he stands, without the gate of stone
Between two walls with silence on them grown,
And littered leaves of silence on the floor;
Here, in a solemn silver of ruined springs
Among the smooth green buds, before the door
He stands and sings.

BOY AND EAGLE

Once upon an adolescent hill
There lay a lad who watched amid the piled
And silver shapes of aircarved cumuli
A lone upcleaving eagle, and the still
Serenely blue dissolving of desire.

Easeful valleys of the earth had been: he looked not back,
Not down, he had not seen
Lush lanes of vernal peace, and green
On ebbing windless tides of trees; no wheeling gold
Upon the lamplit wall where is no speed
Save that which peaceful tongue 'twixt bed and supper wrought.

Here still the blue, the headlands; here still he
Who did not waken and was not awaked.
The eagle sped its lonely course and tall;
Was gone. Yet still upon his lonely hill the lad
Winged on past changing headlands where was laked
The constant blue.

And saw the fleeing canyons of the sky
Tilt to banshee wire and slanted aileron,
And his own lonely shape on scudding walls
Where harp the ceaseless thunders of the sun.

MOTHER AND CHILD

The ship of night, with twilight-colored sails,
Dreamed down the golden river of the west,
And Jesus' mother mused the sighing gales
While Jesus' mouth shot drinking on her breast.

Her soft dove-slippered eyes strayed in the dusk
Creaming backward from the fallen day,
And a haughty star broke yellow musk
Where dead kings slept the long cold years away.

The hushed voices on the stair of heaven
Upward mounting, wake each drowsing king;
The dawn is milk to swell her breast, her seven
Sorrows crown her with a choiring ring;
A star to fleck young Jesus' eyes is given,
And white winds in the dusk-filled sails to sing.

Frances Gibson

I AM TIRED OF BEING I

I am tired of being I.
I should like to be water,
As grey and dusky as a winter cloud,
As gay and dancing as that silver scarf
Of a stream clinging to the pointed stones,
As soft and cool and clear
As those little ponds of water mirroring the sky,
As brown, as smooth, as calm
As those pools laden with soft mud,
As elusive as those tongues of water
Leaping liquid fire in the sun.
If I could stop being I,
I wonder if I'd ever wish to be myself again?

NIGHT RAIN

Night, like a heavy mist,
Drifts along the streets
In a wet silence.
There is not a shadow in the rain;
And the sullen night,
The mists and streaming trees
Have made me drunk
With bitterness.
I have forgotten how the stars gleam
In silverescent points
Behind their screen of clouds,
I can remember only
The little I am,
And ask myself—
Can this be beautiful:
This bitter rain,
This bitter night,
This bitter heart?

SPELL

One dark night I regarded the spring.
She had lost the golden thunder of her sun;
She had lost the emerald fountains of her trees;
She had lost her seven-petaled flame of color—
But all were there.

She had found the scent of jasmine in unseen mists;
She had found the sleeping silver bird that awoke
When the moon shed her crystal moonlight dust
From a cloud.

STORM

The storm laughed a long black laugh
In his cloud house,
And shook all the crystal panes
Loose from his windows
So that they fell
In a million splinters
Of silver rain.

Sanford C. Gladden

THE CHAIN

Each day upon Life's golden thread I string
My memories,—gifts of the days that are past;
Priceless and pure, tarnished and rusted away;
Misshapen and crude, mayhap, or perfect in cast;
Some wet by tears, others aglow with something
Like unto sunshine,—yet each passing day
Finds my string longer, fairer,—a precious thing.

Often I pause in the midst of my toil,
Telling my beads like some anchorite old.
Gently and slowly I move them;—this one
Pulls at my heartstrings,—recalling so well
The beauty and strength of that friendship, begun
So long ago,—now naught but an empty shell.

I move another down,—then let fall
The entire chain;—the beads, fast-moving, form
An iridescent stream of moods,—happiness
Treading close on the black robe of sorrow; storm

Following sunshine; peace concluding all.
Sighing, I pick them up;—with a caress,
Put them aside as the evening shadows fall.

Yvonne Graham

DAFFODILS

If I should stop to think how life had been,
Had our unreasoning love
Been possible—
I'd pause a moment in the conversation
And then go on—
I'd bid two spades and see
Yellow organdie curtains in a kitchen window
And wonder that the daffodils could bloom
(As always)

I know—
How fire in my eyes
Would have met in yours
Cold steel
I know—
And so, I do not stop to think of it—
Instead I say, "Redoubled—yes—
Ah, thanks!—such charming weather. . . . "
And wonder how daffodils could have the heart
To bloom
As always—.

JAPANESE MAGNOLIA

Out of the rain you came
Out of the darkness
Laughing—
Breathless from your walk—
And in your hand you brought
One wet pink Japanese Magnolia
Exquisitely lovely, shell-pink petals
Curling back from white—
And tender fragrance—wet and fresh
 from the rain.
"I brought you something—"
Then blew away again
Into the night.

QUESTION

How long can I sit here
Wide eyes staring through the darkness
Toward that door?
How long before these rising, tearless sobs
Tightening my throat
Choke me to death?
How long before I run through the darkness
Heart pounding wildly
And tear open that door?
Shall I find you there?
Can I wait that long to find you?

TODAY

The biggest role to play,"
I've heard them say,
"Is yours.
You know that of the two,
Inevitably you
Will lose.
You stay
Because today
He has a need for you—
Yours is the bravest, and the biggest
Thing to do."

But they
Who say it do not know I stay
Because I do
Want you—
All I can have of you
Today—
If tomorrow
Your need for me is gone,
And I'm replaced by quiet and peace—
What can I gain by going
Now, and throwing
Away,
Because I cannot have tomorrow,
Today
And yesterday?

Evelyn Hammett

CANA

My drought of life—
Insipid—pale—
Crystal nor silver could avail
To give it savor or bouquet—

And then you came,
O Exorcist,
And made of it
An aromatic vintage fit
For bacchanal or eucharist.

HYMENEAL

Orange blossoms—
   Rare old lace—
Beneath her veil
   Her radiant face—

He waits in glow
   Of tapers dim—
How he adores—
   Her love of him!

VERONICA

I saw Him stumble—faint
Upon the dolorous way—
I saw His muscles ache
Beneath His rugged load—

I saw His bleeding brow—
His aching arms—His straining back—
His agony of tears!

I said, "Lord, let me wipe Thy face—
Thy holy face—now wet
And grimed with bitter blood and sweat!"

But see—my costly handkerchief—
A tiny web of silk and fragile lace—
Was for that blessed, bleeding face
Inadequate!

And yet—today and every day—
He still alone toils Calvary way,
Still agonized and spent—
And I upon my loom of life
Throughout the years
Another fabric weave—
Another handkerchief—
Oh, will it be
Wide for His wounds—
Broad for His bloody sweat—
Soft for His tears—
Worthy at last His lordly face?

VOCABULARY

God of richness
Be not niggardly—
Give me words for autumn—
Words proud flaunting for red of oaks,

A tone of mellow opulence for gold poplar.
Shape my lips to
Vigorous stately syllables for the towering pines
And some idiom full of ancient fragrance
For the spicy scent of their needless.
Grant me
A comfortable Saxon word for the heavy boughs of the cedar—
A hale and blustering utterance for the wind that twists them.
Some Gallic accents gay and debonair
I need for the flutter and scurry of unanchored leaves.
More than all, I crave
Mystic, worshipful phrases
For the joyous death I see
That shall be joyous life.

Donor of gorgeousness!
Crown the gift—
Leave me not mute
With autumn unexpressed.

Harriet Rice Harned

MARCH

I have no love for March! 'Tis cold, like youth.
It stares with naked eyes at unclothed truth.
It turns the thoughts of aged folk to death
With every perfume-laden breath.
I have no love for March;

For March is cruelty in robes of pink.
Beneath the winsome dress, steel armors clink.
In glee, it rapes the conquered form of earth
With bacchanalian mirth;
For March is cruelty.

A vampire soul has March. It coaxes trees:
"Unfold your buds!" Then stabs a freeze.
It runs its silky fingers through the tender grass,
Then prisons each new blade with glass.
A vampire soul has March.

I have no love for March; but youth is hope.
It brings to age its lavender and heliotrope.
Such pagan pranks it plays with earth and sky!
Today—it smiles—and ask me why
I have no love for March.

Jamie Sexton Holme

JOY

Joy is but a tight-rope
You may walk upon.
Out of mist and cobwebs
All its strands are spun.

Balance back and forward,
Run a step or two,
Sway in time to music—
Any tune will do!

Never look behind you
Till the rope is crossed,
Never look before you,
Else you may be lost.

Never look beneath you,
Lest a step you miss.
Joy is but a tight-rope
Over an abyss!

PREPAREDNESS

I know the fate that comes to one
Who gives her whole heart to a child. . . .
Oh, never burden them with love. . . .
The young and arrogant and wild.

Love music; love the written word. . . .
Love things that time will not decay. . . .
But love not wholly living things
That death, or life, may bear away.

Their clinging hands grow hard and strong,
Their hearts are hard as green young fruit;
Their fancy is a rootless growth,
Their love a vine with scarce a root.

I'll give them what they give to me. . . .
A shallow love, a thoughtless duty. . . .
I'll forge my weapons while I'm young,
A blade of truth, a shield of beauty.

Then knowing all too well the fate
That overtakes a jealous mother,
I'll sit surrounded by my shields....
As unprepared as any other.

SONNET

When sluggish years have cooled our fevered blood,
Which then shall warm us with a temperate glow,
And we, who loved the torrent at its flood,
Dip timid feet in its diminished flow—
Shall we, like lesser lovers, be content—
Forgetting all the glory that has passed,
And thankful for some placid joy unspent
By years that squander every joy at last?
Oh, I shall not forget; I shall remember
The rushing tide that swept us from the shore,
And how this hearth that guards the cherished ember
Once knew how loud a raging flame could roar.
Oh, Time, who dulls both passion and regret—
Grant this one boon—that we may not forget!

Arthur Palmer Hudson

SONGS OF MY HOMEFOLKS

(Proem to a Collection of Mississippi Folk-Songs)

Songs of my homefolks, living bonds
    With dim, dead yesteryears
Of forthright knights and tragic brides
    And Old World dreams and fears:

Now knights are squires' or farmers' sons,
    The brides bear humble names,
And bluff chivalric Robin Hood
    Gives place to Jesse James.

Songs of my homefolks, sweet as English lanes,
    And strong as English oak,
Or redolent of Scottish heaths
    And Irish peat-fire smoke:
Homely your smells, and native too,
    As heaven-trees that parch
On sunburnt sandy hills at noon,
    And new-ground fires in March.

Songs of my homefolks, the cuckoo's voice
    Dies out, faint and forlorn,
And loudly caws the garden thief
    That pecks the farmer's corn.
The raven's now an old black crow;
    He spies no knight new-slain—
Merely the carcass of a horse
    A-lying in the lane.

Songs of my homefolks, trolled of yore
    In castle-keep and bower,
In manor hall and peasant cot,
    Wielding your strange old power;
Even yet you're sung at quitting-time
    On lonely hillside farms,
And still by pine-knot fires you lull
    The child in its mother's arms.

Songs of my homefolks, that yielded joy
    And eased man's troubled heart,
That lightened loads with old romance
    And served the lover's part:
With that keen zest that sought you,
    With that deep joy that kenned you,
With that humility that served you,
    To all men I commend you.

Marjorie Jackson

NON CREDO

I have no faith. To what should I give faith?
To love—mere urge to cast my body-seed?
To God—dark idol carved for cravens' need?
To beauty—light-born, light-endangered wraith?
To truth? Where's one can stand up without scathe
To logic's trust? I've found none for my creed,
Nor any man worthy of my least deed,
Nor any meaning in this whirling swathe
Of dusty ether. Laughter's good; and being,
Except for dreams, is good. I shall endure
To put my trust, then, in this lung-breathed breath—
Have faith in sleeping, drinking, eating, seeing?
Not that. For I cannot even be sure
Of faith in the sweet certainty of death.

OXFORD, MISSISSIPPI
In 1922

The old clock rustily roars out the noon
From courthouse tower in center of the town.

The nags hitched to the fence-posts drop ears down
And shift on to the other foot. The tune
Awakes the drowsing dogs on guard, but soon
They slip back into slumber, while the brown
Flies drone and light, then rise and seek to drown
A sprawling negro's snoring loud bassoon.
Will none, then, listen to the old town clock?
He strikes the requiem and funeral dirge
Of a long, lovely past that lies here—dead.
"O, nags! Your sires and dams knew carriage block!
Wake, curs! Of blood once royal!"—Rusty urge!
The black man slaps at flies and shakes his head.

PINES

I've heard that pines go down to meet the sea,
But never have I glimpsed their sombre green
Against the white of breakers. Yet I've seen
Them standing guard in tall, straight dignity
Upon a hill, and then it seems to me
They did not need the diamond-glittered sheen
Of fluking, blue-foamed waves to foil their lean,
Gaunt hardness, or show their strong beauty.
Always they watch, and, watching, breathe a sigh,
As if the duty were a weary woe,
Shift tired arms a moment, then are still.
What dark, impending perils they think lie
Beyond the horizon, I do not know—
I am content with green pines on a hill.

REMEMBRANCE

I did
Not know how sweet
Was youth until I caught
The scent of locust blooms when I
Was old.

TREES IN WINTER

Gaunt, savage warriors,
Wounded to the death,
Fighting fierce battles in the twilight,
Riding full tilt against the sunset,
Hurling their black spears
Into the raging fires of the West.

Fairy filigree,
Snares for the stars.
Sharp javelins
That stab the cold moon.

Gibbering idiots
In the gray dawnlight.
Nameless, restless ghosts
That fidget in the sunlight.

Shadows
That sit
    And wait
        And listen.

WOMAN'S LOVE

This is a part of all I would have told you,
If you had waited till my love was grown
To honesty and trust, till fear was blown
From my virginity by need to hold you:
What boots the niggard-morsel love I doled you?
I am not yours—nor any man's—alone.
A woman's heart is tragically her own.
She may not give, but only seek to mold you
In body-fires until you comprehend
Her ancient need, her stark necessity
For fertile seed—know giving is your part,
Receiving hers. One moment may you blend
With her mere flesh; but, when she sets you free,
Make no presumptuous bargain for her heart.

Muna Lee

DON HENRY

He was born in a land of ponds and willows,
Of gentle slopes and grazing cattle;
And here his gaze cleaves flaming mallows
To plunge in seas like molten metal.
His boyhood knew the kindly shallows
Reflecting back the moon's one petal,
But cobalt water pours in billows
Over these sands where sea pods rattle.
Yet the white-bloomed beachvines pushing over
Shifting dunes where the slim crane dodges,
The three-leaved beachvines, are as a lever

Which pries apart the tight world's edges
And with a sudden force dislodges
Fiery skies from the fiery sedges—
And his soul stares through to fields of clover
He will see no more, and sees forever.

PLANET

This midsea rock set in water as the spinning earth in air,
This planet of the constellated tropical islands where
Each looks across blue ocean as the stars across blue ether,
This rock is our world and we its slaves and lords together.
And history dwindles to a point in time as earth to this point in space,
And one moment captures them both and it is the moment that we face.

PUERTO RICAN HACIENDA

Afternoon in Don Efrén's field
Tastes of honey and cinnamon and cassava root
And is drowsily heavy with yield
Of thickly fledged furrow and groves of wild fruit.
Sun-colored with mango, night-colored with cane,
Pungent with rose-apple, drowsy with water,
It smells of roasting coffee and jasmine and rain,
Of fields plowed by the oxen of old Don Efrén—
And is sultry and still as Don Efrén's daughter.

RICH PORT

This desperately tilted plane of land, our island,
Toppling from its gaunt sea-rooted pillar,

Slanted ever more definitely toward the sea-floor,
Toward that bottomless rift in the floor of Mona Passage,
   Slipping,
        sliding,
             creeping,
                  ever more surely
This doomed beloved rock edging inch by inch with the earthquakes
Toward implacable disaster,
Some day will lurch, will plunge, the long tension ended,
And ceibas and the yellow fortress and the lizards and the market-place,
The wild beauty of mountain cliffs hung with blue morning-glories,
Immaculate cane-fields and the cool breath of coffee-groves,
Thatched hovels and trolley cars and Ponce de Leon's palace,
Flame-trees and tree-ferns and frail white orchises,
My love and your pride,
All, all will lie in crushed indeterminate wreckage for a thousand thousand years
In the crevasse beneath the floor of Mona Passage,
With aeons of sea creatures moving lightly through the heavy masses of water
Far above the shattered nameless shards
That in 1930 were you and I
            And flame-trees and Porto Rico.

TROPIC DAWN

    Dawn, the great flamingo,
      Takes flight above the hill.
    Incredulous, the raven
      Blinks at the east, until

Bright wide pinions flutter
    Across the granite wall,
And down along the river
    Rose-stained feathers fall.

Gladys B. Legg

WASHING DISHES

A little girl stands on a box at the sink.
Her arms are soft and dimpled and pink.
Her eyes look yearningly over the way. . . .
But she washes the dishes and puts them away.

A maiden stands at the window sill.
A youth passes by and her heart stands still.
He lingers there and love holds sway. . . .
She washes the dishes and puts them away.

A young wife stands at the table there.
Never a worry, never a care.
She sings at her work, it is only play
To wash the dishes and put them away.

A mother stands with face so sad
And looks at the place where her little lad
Never again will lie happy and gay. . . .
She washes the dishes and puts them away.

A widow stands by the window pane.
Love and youth will not come again.
Her heart does not sing, but has learned to pray
As she washes the dishes and puts them away.

Catherine Naomi McFarlane

THE MASQUERADE

This life is but a masquerade.
    Cellini souls wear cowls,
A shy heart flaunts a gay cockade,
    And fools are dressed as owls.

The sensitive soul wears a cynic's mask,
    The serious soul a clown's,
And sometimes warrior souls may ask
    For pious hermits' gowns.

All of us here are well disguised,
    Well masked, lest someone see
The soul we are and be surprised—
    As they would be at me,

For a wood-nymph soul wears my cloak of clay,
And a dryad cleaned the house today.

NOVEMBER

Dull grey skies, and a listless rain
    Drifting down.
Pale grey light on sullen faces
    In the town.

Autumn leaves on the half-bare trees,
    Dim, subdued.
Muddy paths and sodden grass
    Earthly hued.

Wet umbrellas, chilly slickers,
    Rain-soaked gowns.
Dull grey skies, and the listless rain
    Drifting down.

A MISSISSIPPI NIGHT

'Tis a desperate night. How the wild wind howls
    with shuddering rush and moan,
Like a host of baleful spirits far into outer
    darkness thrown.
A ghost-gray light, sourceless and wan, pervades
    the murmurous air,
And the forms of witch hags, Sabbat bound, are
    blown in the pale clouds there.
The scant-leaved oak-trees twist and shrink in
    dread of deeds to be,
While the ghost of a mob-lynched Negro hangs
    once more on his gallows tree.
'Tis a hellish night, when evil thoughts oppress
    the minds of all,
A desperate night, when the devil holds the souls
    of men in thrall.

SPRING IS NEAR!

Spring is near! Can't you see it in the blue sky?
Can't you feel it as the wind blows free?
    Even though the air is nipping
    Still old Winter's grip is slipping,
And today a pale spring beauty smiled at me.

Spring is near! Don't you see the jonquils dancing?
And the maples opening out their rosy buds?
   Cardinals and wrens are singing,
   And the geese are northward winging,
And the crocuses have laid aside their hoods.

There's not yet a veil of green on the horizon,
And the distant hills are russet flecked and sere;
   But a low, exciting humming
   Through the universe is running,
And the whole world whispers softly, "Spring is near!"

A CHANT

I am a part of the infinite:
   Part of the swaying of trees,
   Part of the pushing of growing grass,
   Part of the swarming of bees,
   Part of the whisper of falling rain,
   Part of the murmur of streams.
I am a part of the infinite,
   Part of its creative dreams.

Nelle Graves McGill

THE LONELY STARS

Often, when I am isled in loneliness,
Cast, as it seems, upon an empty shore
About which Time's encroaching waters roar,
And I am frightened, faint and comfortless—
I then recall the stars, serene and calm,

And lift my look to theirs, as from the skies
They gaze on earth, as though with God's own eyes—
Their understanding light a healing balm.

The stars are lonely, too. Each in its place
Is fixed, or cloud-like, runs its orbit true;
I, in God's plan, am set in like degree.
And though the stars seem close, abysmal space
Keeps them apart, as it keeps me from you—
Nor is God closer to them than to me.

MUTE

I cannot speak the thoughts
That crowd my throat to aching;
I cannot speak the dreams
That fill my heart to breaking. . . .
Yet when—in spring—I see the pear tree keeping
Her fragrant, snowy tapers lifted high;
Or sometimes, when I watch a baby sleeping,
Or when an old man—smiling—totters by;
Or sometimes, when a butterfly goes winging
Its fragile way across a windy sky;
Or sometimes, when I hear a young girl singing. . . .
It seems that *I must speak, or I shall die!*

MY DAUGHTER DREAMS

The mirror is a shadowed pool
On which her face floats, pale and cool,
A water-lily floating there;
And little ripples of her hair
Glide softly round a brow and cheek
Serenely innocent and meek.

She breathes but as a lily might
On such a pool; her breathing light
Seems breathed upon her—not at all
Her own; her pulses rise and fall
As if some power, moon-remote,
Controlled the tide within her throat.

Nor does her wide, unwavering gaze,
Herself approve, nor yet appraise;
Her rapt eyes, rather, seem to see
Some beauty unperceived by me,
And which her spirit runs to capture,
Her body left in imaged rapture.

*Youth, though quiescent, ever quests
In dreams beyond our walls, nor rests
Content within our love; for youth
Is promise unfulfilled; is truth
Unproven. Youth must seek—nor cease—
Fulfillment, proof, and so find peace.*

She sighs, and at the tremor slight,
Body and spirit reunite;
She moves, and breezes seem to stir
The mirror's pool, the depths of her;
And now she wakes, and with a smile
Comes back to me . . . a little while.

RESERVATION

I answer you that I am all your own,
And yet I know
It is not so;

Because, sometimes, exultingly I feel
Within me rise
A spirit, free and fleet, and strong as steel,
Which, proud, all other ownership denies,
But is, nor ever can be otherwise,
Than mine alone.

So do not ask it, that I give the whole,
The all of me—
It cannot be;
My trust, my love, my life to you I bring,
Yet while I live—
This swift, mysterious, winging, singing thing,
I needs must keep—as my prerogative;
Oh, do not ask it, for I dare not give
To you my soul!

SYMPATHY

When straining horses run to win a race,
I—crouching—ride, the wind across my face;
When one falls headlong—some must fall and lose—
It is my throbbing flesh sustains the bruise.

Or when some bird-man cleaves the crawling light,
And lifts from earth in suave and singing flight,
It is my heart that circles, lifts, and sings,
While I—exulting—feel the surge of wings.

When one breathes sure, to loose a crystal voice,
It is my soul which, freed, I bid rejoice;
And when some artist limns in lucid hue
His dreams, I glory in my dreams come true.

When lovers kiss, and vow by sun above
Their kindred passion, it is I who love;
And when Death chisels into marble Sleep
Someone unknown, unloved—'tis I who weep.

Frederic Francis Mellen

AT NIGHT

I was only lying with my face turned
    Toward the sky
When I found that I was drinking star-dew from
    A blue-shell bowl.

A LUMP OF COAL

I dare not say how long ago
It was; I really do not know;
But in those days the cycad fronds
Scratched deeply into mirrored ponds.
The giant tree-ferns all ablaze
Shed dew into the morning haze.
Amphibians lived there, monster frogs
Were croaking from the sticky bogs.
No bird
Was heard.
The ponds were shoal with leaves and logs.

A lump of coal is all this is,
Quite black, though washed for ages, years;
But even now my mind upheaves
The fossil stench of rotting leaves

And sweating dinosaurs. I hear
The fossil sounds and then I fear
The groaning of the giant frogs,
And dinosaurs among the bogs
Fighting,
Biting,
And stumbling over bloody logs.

SANCTITY

I heard you when you called, my sweet,
    And I am here;
    Now help me brush
Those golden cobwebs from my feet.

Mary Leslie Newton

THE LEVEES

    Will they hold?
Will they hold? we ask each other!
Will the River, swirling down
    Past field and town
Claim for himself the lands he built of old?
    Will they hold,
The levees hold? we whisper to each other!

    If they break!—
Destruction, ruin, in the wake
Of the wild water, rushing past
    Those barriers that seemed

Like God's own hills, set fast
    And ribbed with rock!
    Who ever dreamed
They could not meet the mighty river's shock
    And hold him in at last?
O, ruin, ruin, ruin, in the wake
Of the swift water, if the levees break!

    Will they hold?
Shall we be spared the idle fields that wait
Untilled, after the floods abate
And leave them bare again,—
    Too late,—
Too late for seedtime and for harvest then?—
    The pestilence foretold
In lingering miasmas, summer long?—
    The hand of fate
Laid ruthlessly alike on weak and strong?
    Oh, will they hold?
Lord God of Rivers, will the levees hold?

THE OLD WAYS

Give me the old ways, and the undying hope
That makes the old ways new. The early sun
Shone no more fair on that familiar slope
In spring, on trees where jessamine had run,
Than ours of autumn, though the trees are bare
And stark again, and all the flowers done.
The flashing cardinal still lingers there;
The wind still blows; and still the memories
Of spring and summer with the autumn share

Our hearts, and make the silent ways of these
A mystic forest, full of storied trees.

Give me no new ways, where the spring is green
Forever, but strange faces wait among
Its lavish blossoms; shadows lurk between
The very eye and heart; the glancing song
Of birds falls coldly on the ear that knows
No single cadence it has treasured long.
Give me no new ways, where the summer rose
Has a new perfume; where the mountain bends
With a new curve against the sky, and throws
New shadows where the path, upwinding, ends
In lonely places, desolate of friends.

No, the old ways are dearest and are best;
If only they have room for sun and rain,
And friends to walk beside us. For the rest,—
Our heaven is high enough!—our hearts, again,
Once filled with love, need seek for love no more,
Nor dream that love itself can yet attain
A higher consummation. Where before
We trod, the soil is sacred; those old ways,
Those old familiar ways we walked of yore,
Dim though with autumn's long memorial haze,
Keep yet the hope that lit a thousand days.

PHOEBE

Phoebe folded up her fan;
Phoebe put her roses down;—
Phoebe frowned (as Phoebe can!)
With a most portentious frown!

Wooed and sued by half the town,
Queen of every maid and man,
Phoebe's roses are her crown;
Phoebe's sceptre is her fan.

Fancy, then, if so you can,
What dismay possessed the town,
When, in pique at maid or man,
Phoebe tossed her roses down.

QUEEN ANNE'S LACE

Queen Anne, Queen Anne, has washed her lace
    (She chose a summer's day)
And laid it in a grassy place
    To whiten if it may.

Queen Anne, Queen Anne has left it there,
    And slept the dewy night;
Then waked, to find the sunshine fair
    And all the meadows white.

Queen Anne, Queen Anne, is dead and gone
    (She died a summer's day)
But left her lace to whiten on
    Each weed-entangled way!

THE REED

I bore no purple grape,
No honey for the bee,—
Who dreamt I was the shape
    Of melody?

He broke me from the root;
He wrought upon me long;
Behold! for I bear fruit,—
The fruit of song!

SESTINA OF THE DEAD MOTHER

When I was once a woman, long ago,
When the world did not blur, and when my breath
Lifted this heavy bosom,—was I so?—
I, who remember nothing clear but death?—
Yet there was something earlier, for I know
I heard his voice saying, 'She slumbereth.'

Was it his voice that said, 'She slumbereth?'
—I do not blame him!—all so long ago,—
And he had never died!—how could he know
The little creature that had breathed my breath
Was mine, my own, even to hold in death,
And bear forever in my bosom so!

She lay there by me, warm and breathing,—so,—
Till someone said at last, 'She slumbereth;
The baby must not feel the touch of death!'
—They took my child away!—so long ago
I only can remember how her breath
Was sweet, like violets that I used to know!

They took my child away!—they did not know
They were compelling me to wander so
Till I find her again, and till my breath
Fall on her cheek, and then 'She slumbereth!'

Be said of her, as once, so long ago,
He said it of me, softly, meaning—death.

Yes, they have taken her from me and death!
They keep her gently, but how shall she know
What love she lost, oh, very long ago,
When someone lifted her and held her—so,—
Looked down on me and said, 'She slumbereth!'—
I, from whose very life she drew her breath!

Oh, till I feel again my baby's breath,
I cannot rest, even in this dim death,
Wherein the living say, 'She slumbereth!'
They do not guess its agonies, nor know
The dead are not as are the living, so
Lying at rest, as I lay, long ago!

It was—so long ago! I felt her breath
Pass by me—lightly—so,—then blinding death!—
They took my child, I know!—He said,
'She slumbereth!'

G. Marion O'Donnell

ELEGIE

And must I never know again
the glory of sunlit mornings
and soft winds?

Never hear again
the clatter of slow rain
on rooftops?

Never feel again
the softness of young flesh
at midnight?

And must I be forever
the silent, quiet tenant
of black rooms?

NOCTURNE FOUR

And now
through the unwashed mornings
through the dreary hotness of the afternoons
and the silver dreams of nights
I feel your presence. . . .

Your face hovers
just behind the candle-flame
luring me through the fire. . . .

I smother in the faint perfume
of your hair
on the pillow beside me. . . .

I remember little was said:
the intellectualities have faded
the opinions
the theories have faded.

But through the silver dreams of nights
wrapped in the virginity of the moonlight
I feel your soul: and life is but a plaything
of the wind

William Alexander Percy

AT SEA

Endure, my heart, endure: that is the ultimate courage.
So much is taken, and the rest seems better gone;
Little remains of the fair and wise, of just and simple.
Break but the shackles and the quailing sound is heard
Of anchor chains that break. The harbors of the past,
Silted, have grown too shallow for our deepening keels,
Or we have lost the star that guided to their entrance.
Nothing is compass to our destinies, unless
The very fortitude of that cursed mariner
Who knows no port but death, yet fights the sail and sweats
And holds the rudder true, be of itself a chart
To guide at last his haggard bark, amazedly,
Beneath the samite wall of some moon-vested town
Where towers stand, more tranquil than somnambulists.
Be brother to the mighty mariners, my heart:
So stoutly sail that there should be a silver port.

HOME

I have a need of silence and of stars;
Too much is said too loudly; I am dazed.
The silken sound of whirled infinity
Is lost in voices shouting to be heard.
I once knew men as earnest and less shrill.
An undermeaning that I caught I miss
Among these ears that hear all sounds save silence,
These eyes that see so much but not the sky,
These minds that gain all knowledge but no calm.

If suddenly the desperate music ceased,
Could they return to life? or would they stand
In dancers' attitudes, puzzled, polite,
And striking vaguely hand on tired hand
For an encore, to fill the ghastly pause?
I do not know. Some rhythm there may be
I cannot hear. But I—oh, I must go
Back where the breakers of deep sunlight roll
Across flat fields that love and touch the sky;
Back to the more of earth, the less of man,
Where there is still a plain simplicity,
And friendship, poor in everything but love,
And faith, unwise, unquestioned, but a star.
Soon now the peace of summer will be there
With cloudy fire of myrtles in full bloom;
And when the marvelous wide evenings come,
Across the molten river one can see
The misty willow-green of Arcady.
And then—the summer stars . . . I will go home.

THE LITTLE SHEPHERD'S SONG
(13th Century)

The leaves, the little birds, and I,
The fleecy clouds and the sweet, sweet sky,
The pages singing as they ride
Down there, down there where the river is wide—
Heigh—ho, what a day! What a lovely day!
Even too lovely to hop and play
      With my sheep,
        Or sleep
     In the sun!

And so I lie in the deep, deep grass
And watch the pages as they pass,
And sing to them as they to me
Till they turn the bend by the poplar tree.
And then—O then, I sing right on
To the leaves and the lambs and myself alone!
    For I think there must be
        Inside of me
          A bird!

OVERTONES

I heard a bird at break of day
    Sing from the autumn trees
A song so mystical and calm,
    So full of certainties,
No man, I think, could listen long
    Except upon his knees.
Yet this was but a simple bird
    Alone, among dead trees.

A PAGE'S ROAD SONG
(13th Century)

    Jesu,
If Thou wilt make
Thy peach trees bloom for me,
And fringe my bridle path both sides
    With tulips, red and free,
If Thou wilt make Thy skies as blue
    As ours in Sicily,

    And wake the little leaves that sleep
        On every bending tree—
    I promise not to vexen Thee
    That Thou shouldst make eternally
        Heaven my home;
        But right contentedly,
    A singing page I'll be
    Here, in Thy springtime,
        Jesu.

PROMETHEAN

All day the vultures sit and tear my heart
Among the scorched unearthly tremulous peaks;
All night it heals and grows with mystic art
Pasture again for purple hammering beaks.

How long will days return with latticed light
And brassy plumes upon my side like fleece?
However long, longer still the night,
The healing longer, and the long dark peace.

THE RETURN OF THE LEAVES

    Leaves and the sweet-choired blue;
    And my heart set free again.
    Leaves, leaves and the dew;
    Free, but not free from pain.

    The laughter of June is shed;
    And my heart gives heed again.
    But, ah, for youth that is fled,
    Fled, with all but its pain.

TO. C. P.

Her spirit's loveliness was such
Her body's loveliness I could not see;
I only know her eyes were heavenly blue
That now are grey with tears for me.

Tallulah Ragsdale

THE CUP

I do not think that Percival, the white,
Who bore through life his virgin innocence,
Nor Galahad, who, guiltless of offence,
Was crowned the stainless and the blameless knight—
Felt, either such a joy when on his sight
The Holy Grail's green splendour burned intense,
As guilty Launcelot—sad with penitence—
Who found forgiveness in its veiled light.

Christ, I that am not blameless, may not see
The blinding Grail of perfect happiness
Revealed in cloudless radiance to me;
But for my penitential sorrow's stress,
O, grant the cup may yet to me appear
Though misted by the falling of a tear.

THE LAST GUEST

Wide echoing emptiness and wind-blown space;
Worn thresholds, over which gay troops of dreams
Fled, laughing back, to mock the vacant place,
So stands my heart's house, while the darkness teems.

Night is far spent; Joy's pink wreath faded lies
Brown on the stone-cold floor. A poppy bloom
Mad Passion dropped, I hold to lidded eyes—
'Twere time the last guest left the darkening room.

All of my heart's-house tenants long since fled;
Why should that one pale ghost-guest, Memory,
Where love's last little fire dies dull and red,
Still sit and gaze across the coals at me?

Kitty Reid

DIRGE

Climb into the dogwood,
Shake its branches bare,
Make a wedding dress
I can wear.

Early in the morning
In the greeneyed dew,
Were a hundred pictures
All of you.

Fragrant are the hyacinths
In the thin, spring rain. . . .
Can this be earth on which
I have lain?

I PUT LIFE OFF TILL DEATH

Sometimes I have sat quietly to watch
Life in a blackbird or a muddy river,

Eyes probing deep into a feather's twitch
Or broad water's shiver.

But my quick nerves facilitate response
To stimuli more tangent—oftener I chose
The easy charm of food and talk and laughter
To one of those.

So I put life off till death had turned to dust
My sensate body, in peace then to discry
Where the roots of oak trees go, what shines
Bright behind the eye.

Now I lust for a costly worm-proof casket,
And crave soft silk to warm my silly bones,
Whine for a priest to chant my funeral service,
In cold, important tones.

TO LIZ

Liz never took a husband, but had thirty
Great nieces and nephews to share her love;
Some she nursed and washed when they were dirty,
The rest she left to home and God above.

She was corporeal fairy godmother,
The magic donor of mortal nickels and dimes,
No gift to one was more than to another,
For Liz was guiltless of such tiny crimes.

At seventy she was busier than the bees,
Talked a great deal to a good many people,
Attended Bible studies, talks and teas,
And voted the new church should build a steeple.

Now she sits reading what she thinks is wise,
And holds her book three inches from her eyes.

Jessa Soper

WHEN YOU FALL IN LOVE WITH ME

Oh, when you fall in love with me
You'll think it merely happened so.
I have it planned so carefully
That when you fall in love with me
You'll say, "It's fate—most certainly!"
And I shall say, "'Tis true, I know."
Oh, when you fall in love with me
You'll think it merely happened so.

Aubrey Starke

AFTER TROY

They say that Helen, when the war was done
    And Menelaus took her home to Greece,
Spent long and weary hours in the sun,
    Hating the boredom of domestic peace,
    Making vague plans to bring a quick release
From household duties and the daily care
Of royal rooms and royal duties there.

But Menelaus, eager for his mate,
    Would beg her to forget the bloody fights,
Thinking that love of him should mitigate
    The endless languor and the stupid nights;

While she, recalling all the old delights
Of Trojan life and love in Trojan halls,
Became oblivious of her husband's call.

So passed the days (for Paris slept
   Beneath the city lost in ashes deep),
And months succeeding months in dullness crept
   Until it seemed to Helen that a sleep
   More cruel than death had put her heart to sleep,
And in the sunshine she would weep to see
The children playing in their gaiety.

They say that things went thus for several years
   With Menelaus never asking why,
And Helen still too proud for all her tears
   To tell her husband that the end was nigh,
   That a young captain with a flashing eye
Had caught her fancy, and tomorrow's dawn
Would show her and the stalwart captain gone.

But thus it was she vanished, she whose face
   Had launched a thousand ships and caused the death
Of Greeks and Trojans fighting for her grace—
   Left one last time, took with her in her stealth
   A dashing soldier and the royal wealth,
While stupid Menelaus woke to find
A heavy burden lifted from his mind.

GANYMEDE

   Tired of the games his playmates still pursue
He stands apart and gazes at the sky,
And as old longings conquer him anew

He lifts his arms—in vain: he cannot fly.
But, suddenly, the whir of eagle's wings
Draws near him and the eagle's shadow falls
Across his dreams of sweet and wished-for things
In secret gardens and in kingly halls.

Deep piercing talons seize him and he feels
Earth slip beneath him with his old desires;
Clasped close against the feathered breast he yields
To the strange ecstasy the god inspires
As up he soars, forgetting earth-bound fright,
The rapt companion of the eagle's flight.

Paul M. West

OCTOBER GOLD

I never knew the earth could hold
So much of gold,
Nor did I dream of its vast treasure
Until on this October day
There burst upon my enraptured senses
This fluorescent sea of golden-rod
And multitude of cosmos
Standing yellow in the sun!

ON THE ROAD TO EMMAUS

And on that day we walked down
    to Emmaus
We talked of trivial things;
Of the heat and dust along the way.

I remember Cleopas said the sand got
>   into his sandals.
And I said he should have borrowed Simeon's
>   ass to make the journey;

Then a stranger overtook us!
We knew he was a stranger for he seemed
To know not of the Prophet who had died
And was so shortly risen.

Then he upbraided us and called us fools
>   And slow of heart,
And explained to us the prophets from
>   Moses to Isaias,
And we thought him then a rabbi!

It was evening as we passed the shop
>   of James, the tanner,
And we constrained the rabbi to sup with us.
And as we sat at meat, he broke the bread
>   and gave it us.
We knew him then, and behold it was the
>   Master
Who had walked and talked with us
Along the road to Emmaus.

SOLACE

BEING YOUNG, I said,
I would not be consoled
For loss of love
By God, or man, or maid:
The last bitter dregs of sorrow,

Go down to Hell and sit
Disillusioned, with the
      Damned!

BEING OLD, and having looked on life
With quiet eyes, and known
The finite littleness of men and years,
Having seen the weathering of rocks
And the smoothing of the ridges on the dunes,
I look to the vastness of the seas
And silence of the gray sky
And solace take from these.

TO A CHARMER

Your charm was potent, Circe,
I am now a swine and
Grovel at your feet;

But in a short season
The spell will break—
Again I'll be a man,
Stand upon my feet!

UNREMEMBERED DAYS

I also sing to unremembered days
Which no great joy nor blinding
Sorrow from its fellows set apart:
Days when I idled, well content
And knew a certain peace of mind and
    heart.

Days which unachieving came and went
And on the morrow straightway I forgot!

VERITY

It does not greatly matter
That October's gold and scarlet
Has changed to gray November,
Nor that this bright water
Shall soon run saffron in
The winter twilight;

That another year shall pass
And though all be older
Few will be the wiser;
That even death shall look
With eyes of flame upon the earth
Does not really matter

For there shall still remain unchanged
The spirit of universal Truth.

Stella Muse Whitehead

MARSH HUNGER

I must go back once more to the marshes by the River,
Knowing I need not ever go anywhere else again;
And watch the copper moon-disk slowly, slowly rising,
Clutched in the yearning arms of a tree, edging the lonely
    plain.

Let me sense the deep, deep silence for miles and miles
 around me,
With nothing to need or touch me, nothing to feel or be ...
But the slow insistent lapping of little waters flowing,
On and on in the darkness, out to the waiting sea.

Kummer Wrinn

ANATHEMA

Hate wells up in the embittered soul of one
Who has held ideals and seen them scorned,
Who has brought enthusiasm to the sacred task
And seen it crushed under the tyranny
Of avarice, sloth, conceit, and ignorance
Set on a throne. The heart bleeds to see youth
Fed daily with the revolting swell of "Thus
It is everywhere"; daily confirmed in mediocrity
And narrowness by those who have never seen
The light; by those who require spiritual death
Of all who walk in their midst; insisting
Always that others must sink to their level
Or be outcast, persecuted, scorned for their
Insistence that elsewhere there is a life
Better, not stagnant, not wallowing in its own corruption.
Incest, inbreeding, treachery, lechery;
Prostitution of all that is noble and fine;
Abortion of whatever good that strives to be born;
Strangulation of every cry for the light;
Amputation of every hand that reaches on high!
Ah, how I hate the foul stench of the place
Worse than bestial, for beasts are not beasts by choice.

Stark Young

DAY COMETH

Across the marble ledges of the dawn,
Rose-tinted and gold, like a Venetian's hair,
Day cometh now, and from the argent lawn
Of Paradise leans down upon the air.

And the white Artemis grows pale and fades,
She who with splendour drowns the unbosomed night,
Her twinkling flock asleep, folded in shades;
The larks are singing on the hills of light.

Waken, O lovely eyelids, waken slowly,
The dew on these green slopes trembles for thee;
This morn is one, but Thou art all, and holy,
And holier with the dawns that are to be.

THE CHOICE OF DEATH

In the late night to fall asleep
Having thee so beside me here!
Beyond thy face I see the fields
In shadowy starlight far and near;
Beyond thy breath I hear the wind
Move far-off like some wanderer
That with his soaring passion sets
The wide wings of the world astir.
To look at last on thy still face
Even as the dark seals up mine eyes,
And keep thee yet, though I shall walk
Amid the stars of Paradise.

THE IDEAL

Thou art as alabaster filled with wine
Wherein the sun of summer shineth through,
Tinged with the sound of bees when the rich vine
Shakes down its garlands in the diamond dew.

Thou art a gleaming saint amid the trees
Whereon the holy moonlight lieth white,
In some old garden where the centuries
Trail their long mantles in the silent night.

And songs of lips dead long ago I hear
Of them whose holy dreams were fraught with pain,
And if I have or have thee not, it were,
O saint and shrine, O life in life, in vain!

THERE SHALL BE NO DAY EMPTY OF YOU

There shall be no day empty of you this side of death;
Wherever I go there is no place alone;
Only your departing steps shall show I come
To last sands and hear the great sea moan.

TO A ROSE AT A WINDOW OF HEAVEN

Whoever put you there with her white hand,
Mary, or some one lonely even in bliss,
O rose, upon that golden ledge,
Forever sweet in that bright land,

Look in upon my little Frances there
And say, she is the rose that clambers up
Over my lonely heart and sends
Her darling sweetness on the air.

Rachel Zeller

ROME

Slow leads the light into unborn tomorrows,
Waking the whispers in the land of sorrows.
Into the dusk the sound of echoed marches
Of soldiers passing cold triumphal arches,
And on the streets the busy market vender
Where grandeur walked in all its clarion splendor
And whispers waking in the land of sorrows
Slow leads the light into unborn tomorrows.

TEN MEN

I know ten men that sit and hum
All night long in their dusty tents;
I know ten men that work a sum
In moth-worn, molded cerements.

And one is Passion, and one is Greed,
And one is Sin of Religious Creed,
And one is Vengeance, and one is Vice,
And one is Envy, and one is nice
With the narrow bareness of hackneyed form,
The silly slyness of social scorn.
Regret and Terror and Selfish Pride
Brood deep in the sum they sit beside.
So they sit and hum for long and long
And the sum is never, never wrong.

I know ten men that sit and hum
All day long in their dusty tents.
I know ten men that work a sum
In moth-worn, molded cerements.

BIOGRAPHICAL NOTES ON THE AUTHORS

LEMUELLA ALMOND was born in Water Valley, Mississippi, 1872, with the family name of Garrett; childhood home was Sarepta; married Daniel Almond, and lived near Abbeville for eighteen years and now lives at Oxford; published: *Memories in Amber* (poems), 1929.

ELIZABETH AUSTIN was born in Vicksburg, Mississippi, February 26, 1914; graduated from All Saints' Junior College, Vicksburg, 1933, and is now a junior at Belhaven College in Jackson, where she is majoring in Art and English; her pictures have taken first place at the Mississippi State Fair for several years.

RODNEY M. BAINE, is a student at Southwestern College of the Mississippi Valley, Memphis, Tennessee; home address, Tupelo, Mississippi.

KATHRYN BARINGER was born in New Orleans in 1903; attended New Orleans public schools; graduated from Sophie Newcomb College, 1925; M.A., Tulane University, 1926; head of French Department, All Saints' College, Vicksburg, since 1927.

JULIA S. BLUNDELL was born in Yazoo City, Mississippi, October 17, 1912; graduated from Yazoo City public schools; B.A. and art certificate, Agnes Scott College, Decatur, Georgia, 1933; now doing commercial art work in New York City.

THOMAS T. BRACKIN was born in Smyrna, Tennessee; B.A. Vanderbilt University, 1920; M.A., Vanderbilt University, 1926; graduate study, George Peabody College, Nashville, Tennessee, and University of Chicago; Associate Professor of English, State College, Mississippi, 1926 to date.

NEZZIE JEANETTE BRASWELL was born near Laurel, Mississippi, January 12, 1912; now lives in Hattiesburg, where she attended public school, and was Literary Editor of the school publication.

CALVIN S. BROWN III was born in University, Mississippi, 1909; B.A., University of Mississippi; M.A., University of Cincinnati; studied at University of Wisconsin; Rhodes scholarship to England, 1930-1933; B.A., Oxford, England, 1932; interested in literature, languages, music, chess, jiu-jitsu, and nature study.

LOIS BROWN lives in Memphis, Tennessee, although she is a native of Mississippi; wrote the poems included in this book while living in Greenville.

MAUD MORROW BROWN obtained her B.A. and M.A. degrees, University of Mississippi; seven years professor of Latin and Greek, Agnes Scott College, Decatur, Georgia; married Dr. Calvin S. Brown, 1905; Past State Regent of Daughters of the American Revolution; present home, University, Mississippi.

ALEX HEAD BURNETT received the degrees of B.A. and M.A., University of Mississippi; held a fellowship there in history; travelled extensively in the United States; has written a number of original verses as well as translated others from French, German, and Latin; present home, Ruleville, Mississippi.

MARY EFFIE CAMERON was born in Madison County, Mississippi; B.A. and M.A., University of Mississippi; graduate study, Cornell University; taught English in Colorado Woman's College, Denver, 1931-33; home address, Louise, Mississippi.

CHARLOTTE CHAMPENOIS was born in Meridian, Mississippi; educated in Meridian public schools; graduated with highest honors, Principia Junior College, St. Louis, Missouri; wrote her first verse at the age of ten.

ADA NEILL CLARK was born in Indianola, Mississippi, September 24, 1897; graduated from Indianola public schools in 1914; attended Hollins College, Virginia; married in 1919 Arthur B. Clark, Indianola, Mississippi.

HORACE POLK COOPER was born in Nashville, Tennessee; graduate of Harvard; spends much time in European travel; for fifteen years has taught English and French at Mississippi State College; interested in architecture, sculpture, painting, etching, music, chess, and college sports.

HUBERT CREEKMORE was born in Water Valley, Mississippi, 1907; B.A., University of Mississippi, 1927; graduate work, Yale University and Columbia University; interested in poetry, drama, music and Medieval English; present home, Jackson, Mississippi.

ADELE DE LA BARRE was born in Pass Christian, Mississippi; studied at All Saints' College, Vicksburg, and at Gulf Park College, Gulfport, Mississippi; graduated from Newcomb College Art School, 1927, editing the *Newcomb Arcade* in senior year; taught at Louisiana Tech, 1927-29; teacher of art in Wellesley College, Wellesley, Massachusetts, 1929 to date; married, 1931, True William Robinson; interested in writing poetry and painting landscapes.

WILLIAM FAULKNER was born in New Albany, Mississippi, October, 1897; moved to Oxford, Mississippi, where his father was later connected with the University of Mississippi; attended Oxford public schools and University of Mississippi; joined Canadian Flying Corps and was a lieutenant when armistice was signed; worked for *The State* and *The Times Picayune* in New Orleans; met Sherwood Anderson, who encouraged him to write; returned to Oxford; married, 1929, Mrs. Estelle Oldham Franklin, of Oxford; published: *The Marble Faun* (poems), 1924; *Soldiers' Pay*, 1926; *Mosquitos*, 1927; *Sartoris*, 1929; *The Sound and the Fury*, 1929; *As I Lay Dying*, 1930; *Sanctuary*, 1931; *These 13* (stories), 1931; *Light in August*, 1932; *A Green Bough* (poems), 1933; *Dr. Martino and Other Stories*, 1934.

FRANCES GIBSON was born in Dyersburg, Tennessee, July 29, 1912; left an orphan at the age of nine, and has since lived with grandparents in Vicksburg, Mississippi; attended public schools of Vicksburg and All Saints' Junior College; one year at West Tennessee Teachers College; winner in a number of essay contests as well as poetry competitions; poetry prize in Laurel Falls Contest, 1930; poetry prize at Mississippi State Fair, 1931.

SANFORD CHARLES GLADDEN was born in southeastern Missouri, 1902; lived for some years in various states in the Mississippi Valley; completed preparatory schooling at Batesville, Mississippi; B.S., University of Mississippi, 1924; M.S., University of Kentucky, 1928; spent several years in graduate study and teaching in various Southern colleges and universities; Assistant Professor of Physics, University of Mississippi.

YVONNE GRAHAM was born in Meridian, Mississippi, 1916; a senior at Mississippi State College for Women; home address, Meridian.

EVELYN HAMMETT was born in Fayette, Mississippi; graduate of Whitworth College, Brookhaven, Mississippi; Ph.B., M.A., and further study at University of Chicago; Professor of English, Delta State Teachers College; author of several magazine articles on the teaching of poetry.

HARRIET RICE HARNED was born near Starkville, Mississippi; married Dr. Horace H. Harned, bacteriologist at State College, Mississippi, on which campus they make their home.

JAMIE SEXTON HOLME was born in Hazlehurst, Mississippi; married Peter Hagner Holme, of Denver, Colorado, where they now make their home; published: *Star Gatherer* (poems), 1926; *Floodmark* (poems), 1930.

ARTHUR PALMER HUDSON was born near Kosciusko, in Attala County, Mississippi, May 14, 1892; educated in the public schools of Mississippi; B.S. (1913) and M.A. (1920), University of Mississippi; M.A., University of Chicago, 1925; Ph.D., University of North Carolina, 1930; member of Phi Beta Kappa; Associate Professor of English, University of North Carolina; author or editor of "Ballads and Songs from Mississippi," *Journal of American Folk-Lore,* 1927; *Specimens of Mississippi Folk-Lore* (Ann Arbor, 1928); *Folk-Songs of Mississippi and Their Background* (Smith Research Prize thesis, University of North Carolina, 1930); "Folk-Songs of the Southern Whites," in *Culture in the South* (University of North Carolina Press, 1933); "The Bell Witch of Tennessee and Mississippi" (in collaboration with Pete Kyle McCarter, *Journal of American Folk-*

Lore, 1934); several folk plays, among them *Get Up and Bar the Door*, produced by the Carolina Playmakers and published in the *Carolina Playbook*, 1930; present home, Chapel Hill, North Carolina.

MARJORIE JACKSON was born in Water Valley, Mississippi, 1905; B.A., University of Mississippi, 1925; winner of Brown Poetry Prize, 1923; married Denzil P. Marshall, 1926, and moved later to present home near Lake City, Arkansas; has written much poetry, some short stories; interested in hunting, fishing, music and nature study.

MUNA LEE was born in Raymond, Mississippi, January 29, 1895; attended Blue Mountain College, 1909-10 and University of Oklahoma, 1911-12; B.S., University of Mississippi, 1913; married Luis Munoz-Marin, of San Juan, Porto Rica, 1919; Director Bureau of International Relations, University of Porta Rica; on leave of absence, 1931-32, to act as director of national activities of National Woman's party of U. S., member of the committee on international action, Woman's Party, 1928; a speaker before the Sixth Pan-American Conference, Havana, Cuba, 1928; honorary president of the Liga Social Sufragista of Cuba, 1928; director of the Bureau of Public Relations and Information, Inter-American Commission of Women of Pan-American Union, summers, 1928, 1929; member of the Society of Woman Geographers, Poetry Society of America; awarded lyric prize by *Poetry Magazine*, 1915; published: *Sea-Change* (poems), 1923; contributes to the *Nation, North American Review, Ladies' Home Journal, Bookman* and other periodicals; present home, Condado, San Juan, Porto Rica.

GLADYS BROOKRESON LEGG was born in Buffalo Gap, Texas, June 12, 1893; spent her childhood in Aberdeen, Texas; moved to Mississippi, 1920; Poet Laureate of the Mississippi Federation of Women's Clubs, 1930-31; president of the Second District of the Mississippi Federation of Women's Clubs and a member of the Community Culture Club of Electric Mills, Mississippi.

CATHERINE NAOMI MCFARLANE was born in Aberdeen, Mississippi, October, 1909; graduated from Aberdeen public schools, 1925;

B.A., University of Mississippi, 1929; M.A., University of Mississippi, 1931; fellowship in English, 1929-1931; Assistant to the dean of women, 1929-1931; now student at the School of Social Work of Tulane University.

NELLE GRAVES MCGILL was born in Bloomington, Illinois; attended public schools and Baker University, Baldwin, Kansas; married E. H. McGill; Poet Laureate of the Mississippi Federation of Women's Clubs, 1932; represented Mississippi in an international collection of star poems exhibited by the National Council of Women at the Century of Progress Exposition in Chicago, 1933; interested in music and art; present home, Electric Mills, Mississippi.

FREDERIC FRANCIS MELLEN was born in A. & M. College, Mississippi, where his father was a professor; B.A., State College, Mississippi; present home, Starkville, Mississippi.

MARY LESLIE NEWTON was born in 1874; attended University of Tennessee; M.A., Columbia University, 1908; dean of All Saints' College, Vicksburg, September 1916 to date.

G. MARION O'DONNELL was born in Midnight, Mississippi, 1914; spent short time in New York, but has spent the greater part of her life on Blue Ruin Plantation, at Belzoni, Mississippi; temporarily living in Memphis, Tennessee, and editing *The Observer,* a literary magazine publishing work by Southern writers and Europeans of modern tendencies.

WILLIAM ALEXANDER PERCY was born in Greenville, Mississippi, May 14, 1885; A.B., University of the South, Sewanee, Tennessee, 1904; LL.B., Harvard, 1908; unmarried; has practiced law at Greenville since 1908; with Commission for Relief in Belgium, 1916; served with A. E. F. in France; honorable discharge as captain in 1919; published: *Sappho in Levkas,* 1915; *In April Once,* 1920; *Enzio's Kingdom,* 1924; *Selected Poems,* 1930; editor, *Yale Series of Younger Poets;* home, Greenville, Mississippi.

TALLULAH RAGSDALE is a poet and novelist; published: *Miss Dulcie from Dixie* (novel), 1919; *If I See Green* (poems), 1929; present home, Brookhaven, Mississippi.

KITTY REID was born in Greenville, Mississippi; attended school there.

JESSA SOPER attended the public schools of Greenville, Mississippi, in which city she still lives.

AUBREY STARKE was born in Water Valley, Mississippi, October 31, 1904; moved to McComb, Mississippi; B.A., Harvard University, 1927; taught English at Harvard and Northwestern University, Evanston, Illinois; gave up teaching to write; present home, Centralia, Illinois.

PAUL MONTREVILLE WEST was born in Baird, Mississippi, February 8, 1902; attended Sunflower County Agricultural High School, Moorhead, Mississippi and Mississippi A. & M. College; B.S., Delta State Teachers College, Cleveland, Mississippi, 1929; M.A., George Peabody College for Teachers, Nashville, Tennessee, 1930; graduate work, George Peabody College; instructor in English, Delta State Teachers College and, during summer sessions, George Peabody College; dean, Sunflower Junior College, 1930 to date; writer of miscellaneous poems and short stories; published: *Myths and Legends of the Mississippi Indians* (1920).

STELLA MUSE WHITEHEAD was born in Savannah, Georgia; lived for short time in Minneapolis, Minnesota; has lived in Mississippi since 1923; studied voice for eight years in the North and South; present home, Tupelo, Mississippi.

KUMMER WRINN, pseudonym.

STARK YOUNG was born in Como, Mississippi, October 11, 1881; B.A., University of Mississippi, 1901; M.A., Columbia University, 1902; unmarried; instructor in English at the University of Mississippi, 1904-1907; instructor in English literature, 1907-10, and professor of general literature, 1910-15, University of Texas; professor of English, Amherst College, 1915-21; member of the editorial staff of the *New Republic;* lecturer in Italy for Westinghouse Foundation,

1931; published: *The Blind Man at the Window* (poems), 1906; *Guenevere* (play in verse), 1906; *Madretta, Addio, The Twilight Saint, The Seven Kings and the Wind, The Queen of Sheba, The Dead Poet, The Star in the Trees* (one-act plays in prose and verse), 1911; *Three Plays,* 1919; *The Flower in Drama* (essays on the theatre), 1923; *The Three Fountains,* 1924; *Sweet Times and the Blue Policeman* (plays for children), 1927; *The Colonnade,* 1927; *Rose Windows* (one-act plays), 1927; *Glamour* (essays that contribute to the theatre arts), 1927; *The Torches Flare* (novel), 1927; *River House* (novel), 1929; *The Street of the Islands* (short stories), 1930; divers articles in periodicals; present home, New York City.

RACHEL ZELLER is a native of Yazoo City, Mississippi; B.A. and M.A., University of Mississippi; Brown poetry prize, 1926; teacher of English and Latin, University High School, Oxford, Mississippi, 1930-31; now doing social service work in Philadelphia.

www.ingramcontent.com/pod-product-compliance
Lightning Source LLC
Chambersburg PA
CBHW030118010526
44116CB00005B/303